Sam McCool's New

PITTSBURGHESE

Sam McCool's New
Pittsburghese
How to Speak Like a Pittsburgher

by Sam McCool

Cover Photo by: Thomas R. Pollard
Illustrations by: Dave Hereth/New Image Press

To Jean Lam and Paul Thompson I owe a great deal for advice and encouragement. Without their push the book may have been forgotten and this edition would never have been done. Finally, there are many Pittsburghers, some living far from home, who deserve much thanks for their kind letters of praise and appreciation, and for not punching me in the nose.

A

Ahia: the state west of Pennsylvania; also, a major thoroughfare into the City. "Morning rush-hour traffic is always heavy on East *Ahia*."

Aht: some place, like the mall or the corner drugstore, just to spend time and sometimes money – "I'll see you later, I'm going *aht*!"

Aht aht: a heavy date; much more serious than just *aht* – "Don't wait up, I'm going *aht aht.*"

Ahz: an unusual form of "I am" as in "*Ahz* sick n' tired of this place."

Alright: well, fine; used most often as a reply to "How are You?" *"Alright."*

Anymore: signifies a prevailing condition or situation, as in "*Anymore* there's so many new buildings, you can't tell which is which."

Arn: a popular beverage, Iron City Beer. "There's nothing like a cold *Arn.*"

Ats: that is – "*Ats* what I'm trying to tell you."

B

Babushka: a colorful, patterned scarf, commonly worn by women while shopping or spring cleaning.

Bahks: a container, usually cardboard; sometimes the act of packing a container, as in "Most downtown stores will *bahks* gifts at Christmas."

Blahse: worn by most women anytime – "Is that pretty *blahse* new?"

Bloomfilled: an east end community. "Whatever happened to the *Bloomfilled* Bridge?"

Boilermaker: a combination of whiskey and Iron City, dropping the shot glass into the beer. Do not confuse with an "Imp 'n Arn" or "Shinley 'n Arn."

C

Cahch: a piece of furniture usually found in the livingroom. "Dad's asleep on the *cahch* again."

Carbon oil: a flammable, smelly fuel, known also as kerosene.

Carline: the tracks on which "streetcars" or trolleys run. "The drugstore is conveniently near the *carline.*"

Caw: trying to get somebody's attention; or, telephoning him, as in "I *cawd*, but you weren't home."

Chipped-chopped ham: processed ham, sliced paper thin – "The deli has *chippedchopped* ham on sale; I hope some is left."

Chitchat: conversation, usually on the telephone about nothing in particular – "Call me later, and we'll *chitchat*."

City chicken: has nothing to do with chicken; instead, a combination of breaded veal and pork skewered and grilled.

Couttent: could not, as in "I *couttent* make it on time, 'cause the streetcar broke down."

Crewsants: a cheesey, crescent shaped pastry, popular in the east end. "I can't get started without coffee and a *crewsant.*"

Cuboard: a closet for storing coats, hats, babushkas, etc. "Hang your coat in the *cuboard.*"

D

Dahntahn: below uptown. "*Dahntahn* is still a great place to shop."

Dawn: a popular man's name – Don or Donald. "*Dawn* and *Rawn* are still good friends."

Dill: deal, as with cards, not pickles, unless it's a good *dill* of them. "I know a good *dill* when I seen one."

10

Dittent: did not, as in "I *dittent* do my homework, did you?"

E

Et: one of the necessary human interruptions of the course of world affairs. "I haven't *et* yet, I've been so busy."

F

Fahnd: to discover or locate – "You'll *fahnd* a lot of friendly people in Pittsburgh."

Fahr: the oxidation of materials, accompanied many times with flame and smoke. "There's a four alarm *fahr* on the South Side."

Fell: the opposite of succeed, as in "I *felled* my driver's test again."

Filled: a large open space, as in "The Pirates used to play in Forbes *Filled.*"

Filum: used in most cameras, essential to good vacations. "Make sure we have *filum* for the camera."

Flahr: a cherished sign of spring, as in "A *filled* of *flahrs.*"

G

Gommed up: filthy, dirty from end to end. "That child has himself all *gommed up.*"

Grinny: a small wild animal common in Pennsylvania; also known as a chipmunk.

Gumbans: pieces of soft elastic rubber, occasionally used to keep trouser cuffs out of bicycle chains, or papers from flying around in your brief case. "Where are the *gumbans* and paper clips?"

H

Hans: they usually get red and rough during Pittsburgh winters. "We need a good pair of *hans* to help fix our leaky roof."

Hap: a comforter or quilt, as in "I need my *hap* to take a nap."

High hills: high heels, as in "She's wearing *high hills* to the prom."

Hoagie: a submarine sandwich, heated and spicy.

How's about: how about, but so much more effective with the "s." *"How's about going out tonight?"*

I

Imp 'n Arn: a popular beverage combination – a shot of Imperial chased with Iron City beer.

I 'n near: Eye and Ear Hospital – "Maybe you ought to enter *I 'n near.*"

In regards to: a wordy expression, attempting to make the speaker sound intelligent, as in "*In regards to* the recent speculative activity on Wall Street..."

J

Jaggers: thorns – "Watch, there's *jaggers* on that plant!"

Jaynell: Jones and Laughlin Steel Co. "The *Jaynell* mill along Second Avenue is a well known Pittsburgh landmark."

Jeet jet: not a supersonic; rather, an inquiry heard frequently around lunch time – *"Jeetjet?"* "No, j'ew?"

Jynt Igl: a popular grocery store chain. "I need a few things at *Jynt Igl.*"

Jumbo: bologna. When a Pittsburgher orders a *jumbo* sandwich, he is not ordering a large sandwich.

K

Keller: color, as in "I hate the *keller* but it's a nice car."

Klondike: a popular ice cream treat, known to have been air-lifted to distant parts of the United States by dislocated Pittsburghers hooked on its unique taste.

L

Leave: let or allow, as in "If you clean your room, Mom will *leave* you go to the movies."

Lenth: length, as in "There's a line the *lenth* of a block waiting to get in the Stanley."

Living daylights: a figurative expression usually refering to a beating, as in "He beat the *living daylights* out of opposing linemen."

M

Mill: food, a meal – "That was a good *mill,* Mom."

Mon: the Monongahela River. "Cross the *Mon* at Birmingham and you'll be on the South Side."

N

Nebby: nosey as in "Aunt Edie is so *nebby* nobody can stand her."

Needs: used for "needs to be" as in "The car *needs* washed."

Nize: nice, as in "I'm looking for a *nize* warm coat for winter."

O

Onion snow: a light, late spring snow, just enough to cover the ground but not hide the onion shoots.

P

Pahn: pound. "Give me a *pahn* of chippedchopped ham."

Pensivania: the state in which true champions find Pittsburgh.

Perch: porch – where Pittsburghers spend quiet summer evenings drinking Arn and chitchatting.

The Point: Point State Park, found downtown at the meeting of the Allegheny and Monongahela Rivers.

Pop: cherry, orange, root beer and other carbonated beverages – "I'll have a burger, fries, and *pop.*"

R

Redd up: clean or tidy an area as in "Quick, *redd up* the house, Mom is coming."

Reverend: great, extreme, as in "You can tell he hasn't bathed for days by the *reverend* odor."

Rilly: really – "Pittsburghers think Klondikes are *rilly* good."

S

Sahside: a neighborhood of the City, across the Mon, known for steel mills, paper suppliers, warehouses, cement, and tough kids.

Sammitches: a quick meal – "Mom's making jumbo *sammitches.*"

Scrub: wash or clean, as in "My hair needs *scrubbed.*"

Skworuhill: an east end community well known for kosher deli's, great pizza, Poli's, and beautiful homes.

Sleep in: to sleep late – "I like to *sleep in* Saturday."

'Sliberty: an east end community known for its Highland Mall and beautiful churches.

Slippy: slippery. "Watch your step, the sidewalk's *slippy.*"

Spicket: tap or spiggot. "When are you going to fix the hot water *spicket?*"

Still: a metal for which Pittsburgh is famous. "Remember the good old days when they used *still* to build cars?"

Stillers: Pittsburgh's champion football team. "The *Stillers* are tough."

Stillmill: where "still" is made. "Pittsburgh has many *stillmills.*"

Stogie: a cigar, now used for any cigar, but originally a long, thin cigar associated with Conestoga drivers and manufactured in Pittsburgh.

Streecar: streetcar or trolley – "Why hurry, we'll only have to wait on the *streecar?*"

Strenth: strength.

Strip District: or the Strip – wholesale markets, warehouses, supply depots, etc. "I like shopping for vegetables early mornings in the *Strip.*"

T

Tahl: towel, as in the "*terrible tahl.*"

U

Uptahn: above   "dahntahn." "You'll hear Pittsburghese spoken *uptahn.*"

W

Wait on: wait for, as in "I had to *wait on* the bus for a half hour this morning."

Wants: used for "wants to be" as in "The customer *wants* served."

What the cat drug in: a figurative expression, usually to describe a person's appearance. Formerly longer – "What the cat drug in and the dog wouldn't eat."

Whenever: an indefinite time, literally "when" – *"Whenever* I finish the car, I'll take you for a ride."

Willer: the Wheeler School.

Worsh: wash, or the clothes which have been *worshed,* as in "The *worsh* froze on the line, so you'll have to wait for your trousers to defrost."

Y

Yock: the Youghioghenny River.

Yunz: all of you, literally "you ones." "Are *yunz* going to the game?"

The Author

A resident of Pittsburgh's Brighton Heights, Sam McCool has a B.A. from the University of Pittsburgh and a M.A. from West Virginia University, both in English literature. When he's not putting friends and acquaintances to sleep with tales of seafarers and discourses on irregular Anglo-Saxon verbs, he practices his Pittsburghese.